I CAN BOWL!

Written by Linda Johns
Illustrated by Jim Caputo

Children's Press®
A Division of Scholastic Inc.
New York • Toronto • London • Auckland • Sydney
Mexico City • New Delhi • Hong Kong
Danbury, Connecticut

For Theo
—L.J.
To Janet, Mami, and Papi
—J.C.

Reading Consultants

Linda Cornwell
Literacy Specialist

Katharine A. Kane
Education Consultant
(Retired, San Diego County Office of Education and San Diego State University)

Library of Congress Cataloging-in-Publication Data

Johns, Linda.
   I can bowl! / written by Linda Johns ; illustrated by Jim Caputo.
      p. cm. — (Rookie reader)
   Summary: When a boy and his mother go bowling, he demonstrates how to play the game.
   ISBN 0-516-22374-7 (lib. bdg.)   0-516-27496-1 (pbk.)
   [1. Bowling—Fiction. 2. Mothers and sons—Fiction. 3. Stories in rhyme.] I. Caputo, Jim, ill. II.
Title. III. Series.
   PZ8.3.J622 Iae 2002
   [E]—dc21
                                2001008348

CHILDREN'S PRESS, AND A ROOKIE READER®, and associated logos are trademarks
and or registered trademarks of Grolier Publishing Co., Inc. SCHOLASTIC and
associated logos are trademarks and or registered trademarks of Scholastic Inc.

1 2 3 4 5 6 7 8 9 10 R 11 10 09 08 07 06 05 04 03 02

Cool shoes!
I slip and slide.

3

**This wood floor
helps me glide.**

Bowling ball
smooth and round.

Ugh! It's heavy.
It weighs six pounds!

Ten pins lined up
straight and tall.
What's my job?
Make them fall!

I roll the ball.
It starts to sputter.

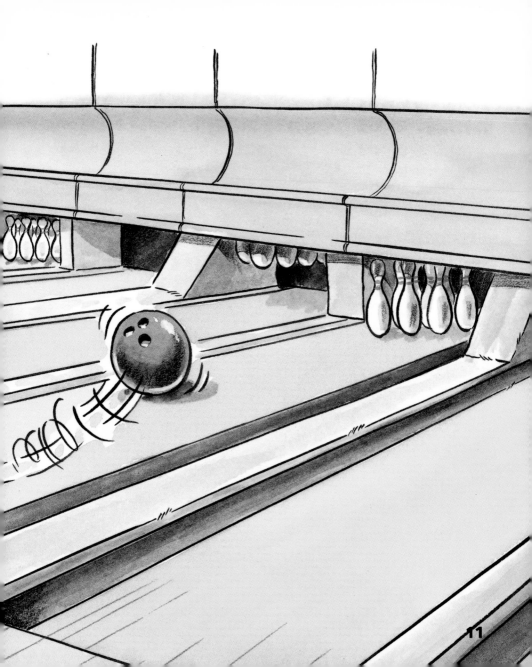

Wobble! Ker-PLUNK!
It's in the gutter!

"This will keep your ball rolling!"

Fences up.
I'm bumper bowling!

I roll the ball.
I knock down four!

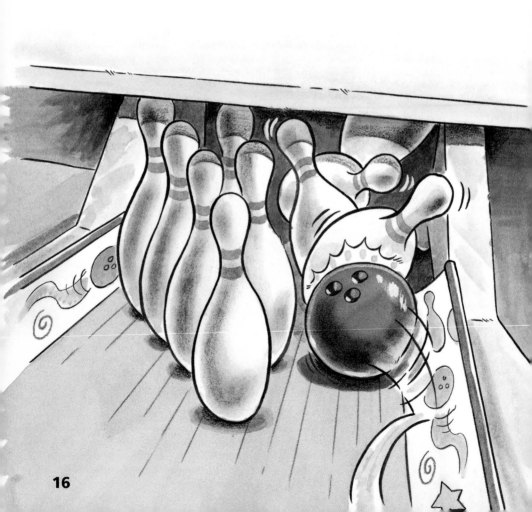

I roll again.
I get two more!

I check the screen.
I see my score.

All right!
I can bowl once more.

I look ahead.
I concentrate.

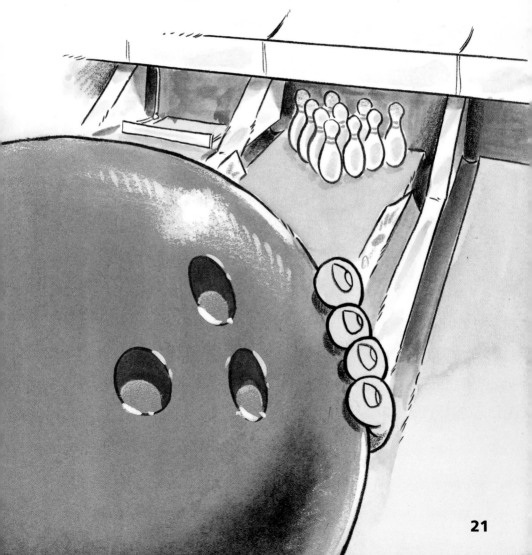

I roll the ball nice and straight.

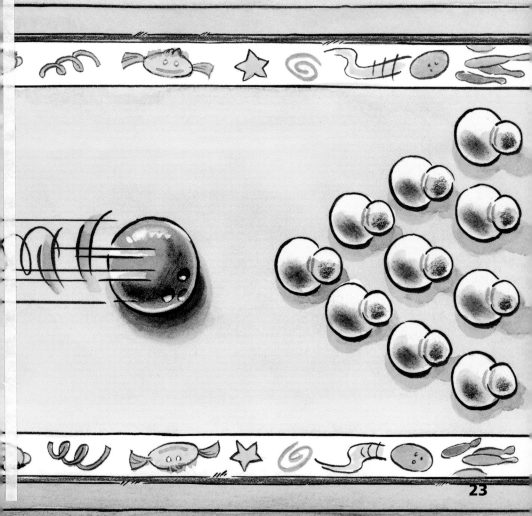

I close my eyes.
I don't want to see.

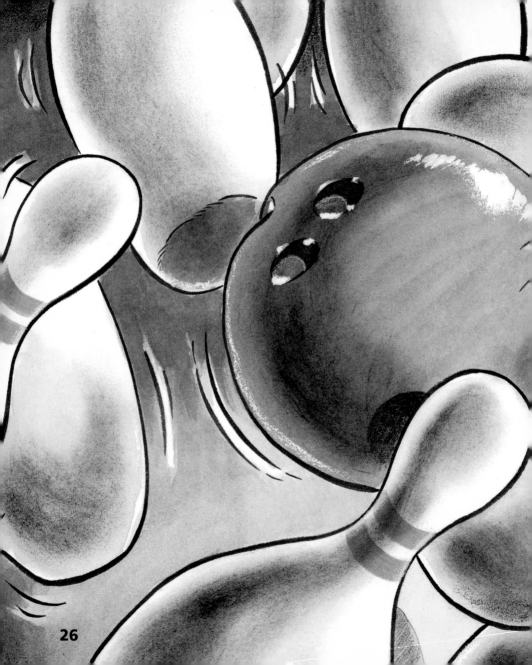

"Strike!"
my mom yells to me.

What?
I got all ten?

I can't wait to bowl again!

Word List (82 words)

again	fall	ker-plunk	score	to
ahead	fences	knock	screen	two
all	floor	lined	see	ugh
and	four	look	shoes	up
ball	get	make	six	wait
bowl	glide	me	slide	want
bowling	got	mom	slip	weighs
bumper	gutter	more	smooth	what
can	heavy	my	sputter	what's
can't	helps	nice	starts	will
check	I	once	straight	wobble
close	I'm	pins	strike	wood
concentrate	in	pounds	tall	yells
cool	it	right	ten	your
don't	it's	roll	the	
down	job	rolling	them	
eyes	keep	round	this	

About the Author
Linda Johns likes any lanes at Leilani Lanes—as long as the bumpers are up. She lives in Seattle, Washington.

About the Illustrator
Jim Caputo is a terrible bowler. He's also an art director and illustrator for a design studio in Orlando, Florida. This is Jim's fourth children's book. In his spare time, he enjoys reading, physical fitness, going to the movies, and spending time with his two dogs, Lumi and Donovan, for inspiration. Unfortunately, all of the inspiration in the world hasn't helped his bowling skills.